A WEE BOOK OF
IONA POEMS

A WEE BOOK OF
IONA POEMS

Kenneth Steven

wild goose
publications www.**iona**books.com

© 2015 Kenneth Steven

First published 2015 by
Wild Goose Publications, Fourth Floor, Savoy House,
140 Sauchiehall Street, Glasgow G2 3DH, UK,
the publishing division of the Iona Community.
Scottish Charity No. SC003794. Limited Company Reg. No. SC096243.

ISBN 978-1-84952-423-0

Overseas distribution
Australia: Willow Connection Pty Ltd, Unit 4A, 3–9 Kenneth Road,
Manly Vale, NSW 2093
New Zealand: Pleroma, Higginson Street, Otane 4170,
Central Hawkes Bay
Canada: Bayard Distribution, 10 Lower Spadina Ave., Suite 400,
Toronto, Ontario M5V 2Z2

Printed by Bell & Bain, Thornliebank, Glasgow

This wee book is for Cecile and John

Introduction

I am not a writer of strict haiku and never will be. These pieces, or fragments, represent moments from many Iona days: distillations of memories. They happen to us all, I believe: moments when we slip out of 'everydayness' into somewhere beyond. And perhaps that happens more often on this island that has been special to people for so many centuries, where a sense of the divine has felt closer in what George MacLeod called 'a thin place' …

– Kenneth Steven

After the storm

blue sky comes back —

a whole field of sunlight.

A little glen

opens its winter dark

into the riches of orchids.

There is a beach

where globes of Baltic amber can be found:

hold them in the sun like honey.

The marble quarry

is never where you want it to be —

I'm sure they move it in the winter.

Before nightfall

the Ross of Mull

left bloodstone by the sun.

Sometimes

it's about little more

than a boat on a blue sea.

Straggled and limping

a skein of greylag geese –

voices like bagpipes.

Ten thousand people come here every day

the whole of July and August.

Cross to the west side and there's silence.

A single canoe

needles and sews

the Sound of Iona.

There are Hebridean songs

made just so the seals

will break the skin of the sea.

A new morning:

another miracle

we fail to see.

Two ravens

playing in the wind

and talking nonsense.

An otter

made of so much sea

flows over stone, solidifies.

A man

fights his way against the wind

going nowhere.

A gannet

made of faith

gimlets the sea.

Across the stone
old as Columba
feet whisper prayer.

A moon

looks out of the low sky

lighting the way.

A piece of Ireland

worn down

to nothing more than light.

The last ferry's gone —

a drawbridge has been lifted

and the island left behind.

Another shoal of tourists

spills out across the jetty:

a good catch today.

Otters can't be ordered

they happen by accident

when you least expect them.

At Columba's Bay

throw one stone into the sea –

something you want to leave behind.

It must have been a dreich day

when Columba landed on Iona:

you *can* see Ireland from the summit of Dun I.

Five goldfinches

strung out on the telegraph wires:

notes in the storm's tune.

At the Hermit's Cell

if you sit and listen

all you will hear is silence.

Look at the light

there on the top of the ridge:

the angels are dancing.

Spring comes at last

with armfuls of daffodils and lambs;

only Ben More still wears a skullcap of snow.

A lark

no larger than a man's hand

sings the whole sky.

An eagle bending

in a single bar of gold

over the top of Dun I.

There are no shortcuts through bogs

just lost shoes

and wet homecomings.

Not a breath of wind

this late August night:

the midges are dancing a jig.

A full moon tonight:

bright enough to walk the whole way

through the Glen of the Temple and back.

Sometimes

it takes a long time

to learn you can be wrong.

I find God

when I come back here

and stop looking.

Also by Kenneth Steven:

The Monk and the Mermaid
A story from Iona, told for children

On St Columba's Bay at the south end of the island of Iona, the beach where the monks first landed in their coracles from Ireland, you can still find the most beautiful green stones, polished by the sea. This is the legend, told for children, of how these wonderful stones came to be, and why they are there to this very day.

24 pages with colour illustrations and text
ISBN 9781849522014

Wild Goose Publications is part of the Iona Community:

- An ecumenical movement of men and women from different walks of life and different traditions in the Christian church
- Committed to the gospel of Jesus Christ, and to following where that leads, even into the unknown
- Engaged together, and with people of goodwill across the world, in acting, reflecting and praying for justice, peace and the integrity of creation
- Convinced that the inclusive community we seek must be embodied in the community we practise

Together with our staff, we are responsible for:

- Our islands residential centres of Iona Abbey, the MacLeod Centre on Iona, and Camas Adventure Centre on the Ross of Mull

And in Glasgow:
- The administration of the Community
- Our work with young people
- Our publishing house, Wild Goose Publications
- Our association in the revitalising of worship with the Wild Goose Resource Group

The Iona Community was founded in Glasgow in 1938 by George MacLeod, minister, visionary and prophetic witness for peace, in the context of the poverty and despair of the Depression. Its original task of rebuilding the monastic ruins of Iona Abbey became a sign of hopeful rebuilding of community in Scotland and beyond. Today, we are about 250 Members, mostly in Britain, and 1500 Associate Members, with 1400 Friends worldwide. Together and apart, 'we follow the light we have, and pray for more light'.

For information on the Iona Community contact:
The Iona Community, Fourth Floor, Savoy House, 140 Sauchiehall St, Glasgow G2 3DH, UK. Phone: 0141 332 6343
e-mail: admin@iona.org.uk; web: www.iona.org.uk

For enquiries about visiting Iona, please contact:
Iona Abbey, Isle of Iona, Argyll PA76 6SN, UK. Phone: 01681 700404
e-mail: ionacomm@iona.org.uk

Wild Goose Publications, the publishing house of the Iona Community established in the Celtic Christian tradition of Saint Columba, produces books, e-books, CDs and digital downloads on:

- holistic spirituality
- social justice
- political and peace issues
- healing
- innovative approaches to worship
- song in worship, including the work of the Wild Goose Resource Group
- material for meditation and reflection

For more information:

Wild Goose Publications
Fourth Floor, Savoy House
140 Sauchiehall Street,
Glasgow G2 3DH, UK

Tel. +44 (0)141 332 6292
Fax +44 (0)141 332 1090
e-mail: admin@ionabooks.com

or visit our website at
www.ionabooks.com
for details of all our products and online sales